This Book Belongs To

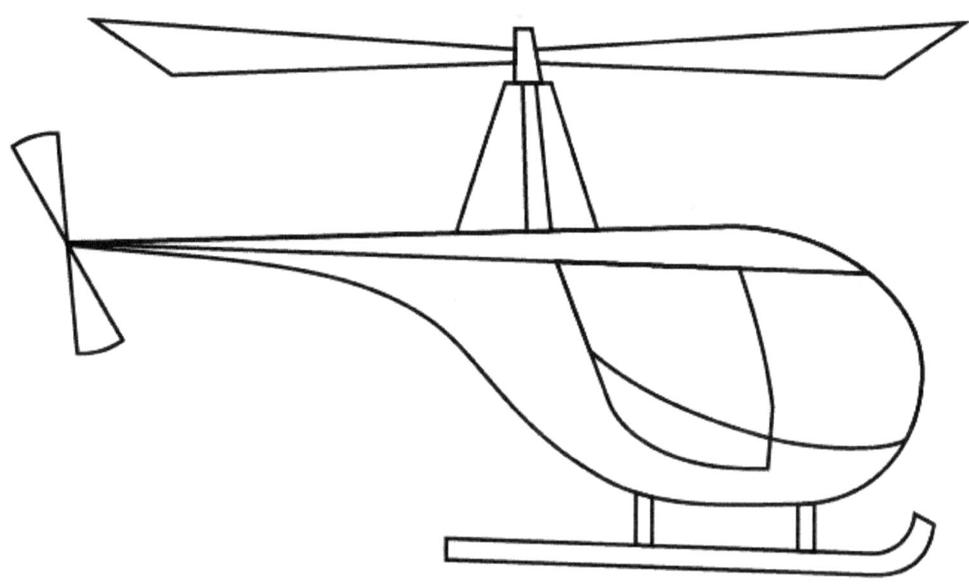

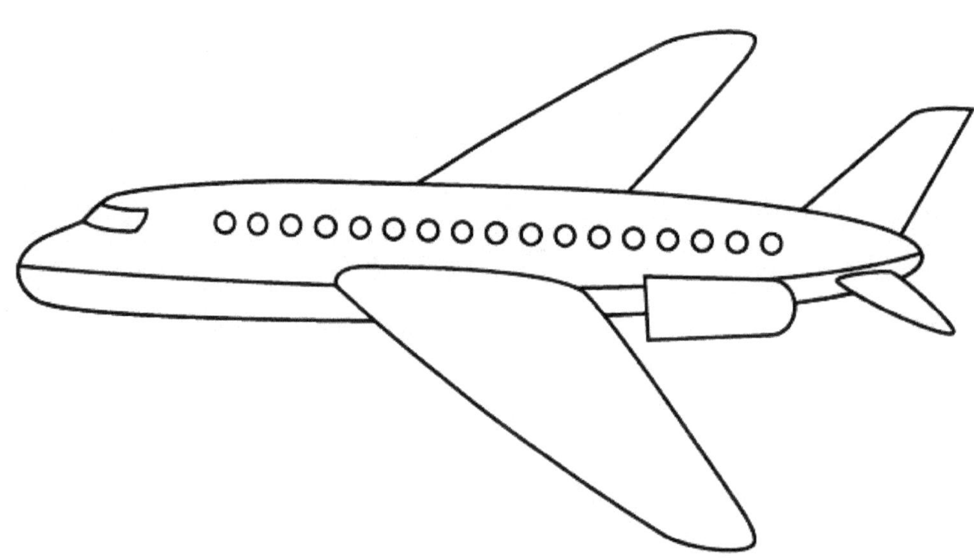

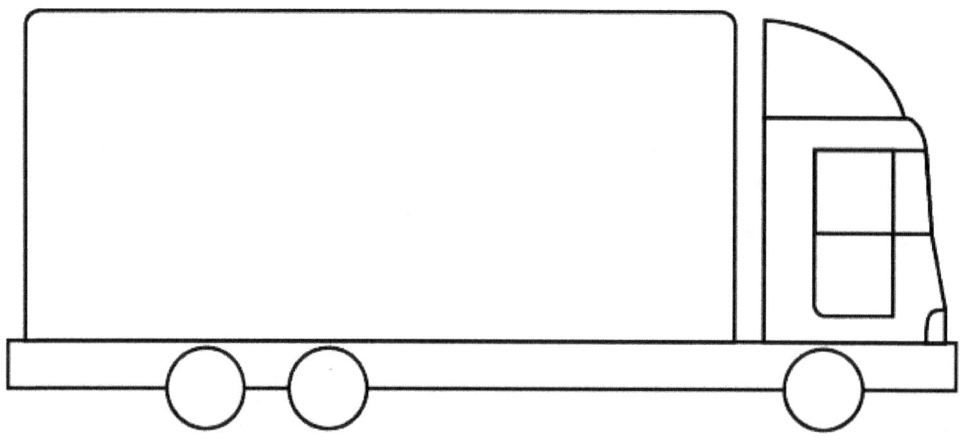

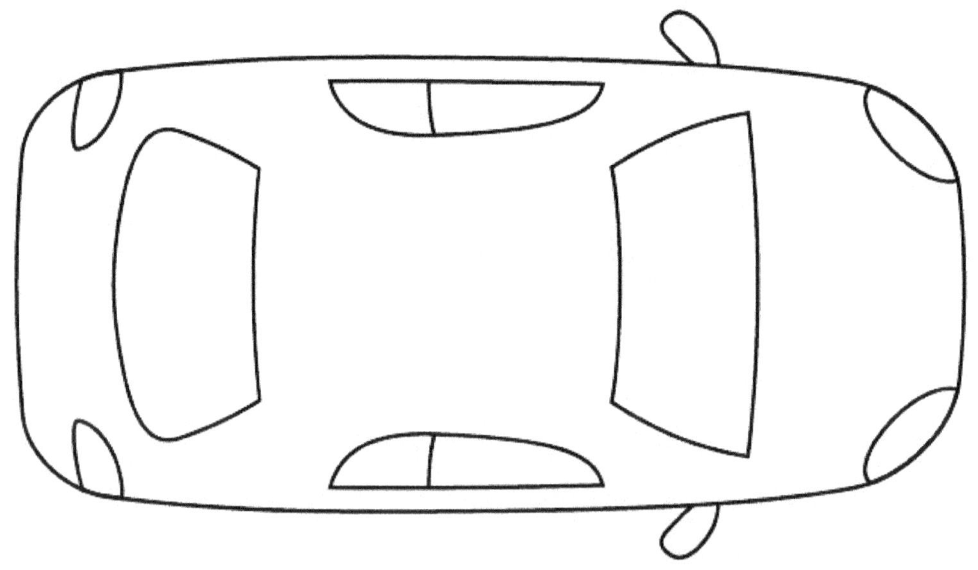

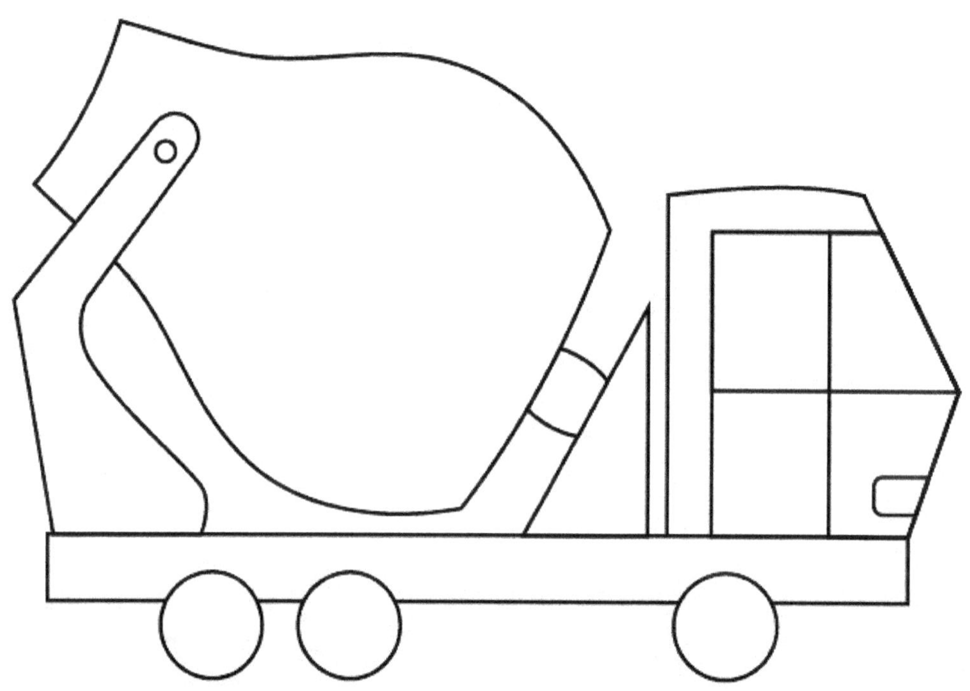

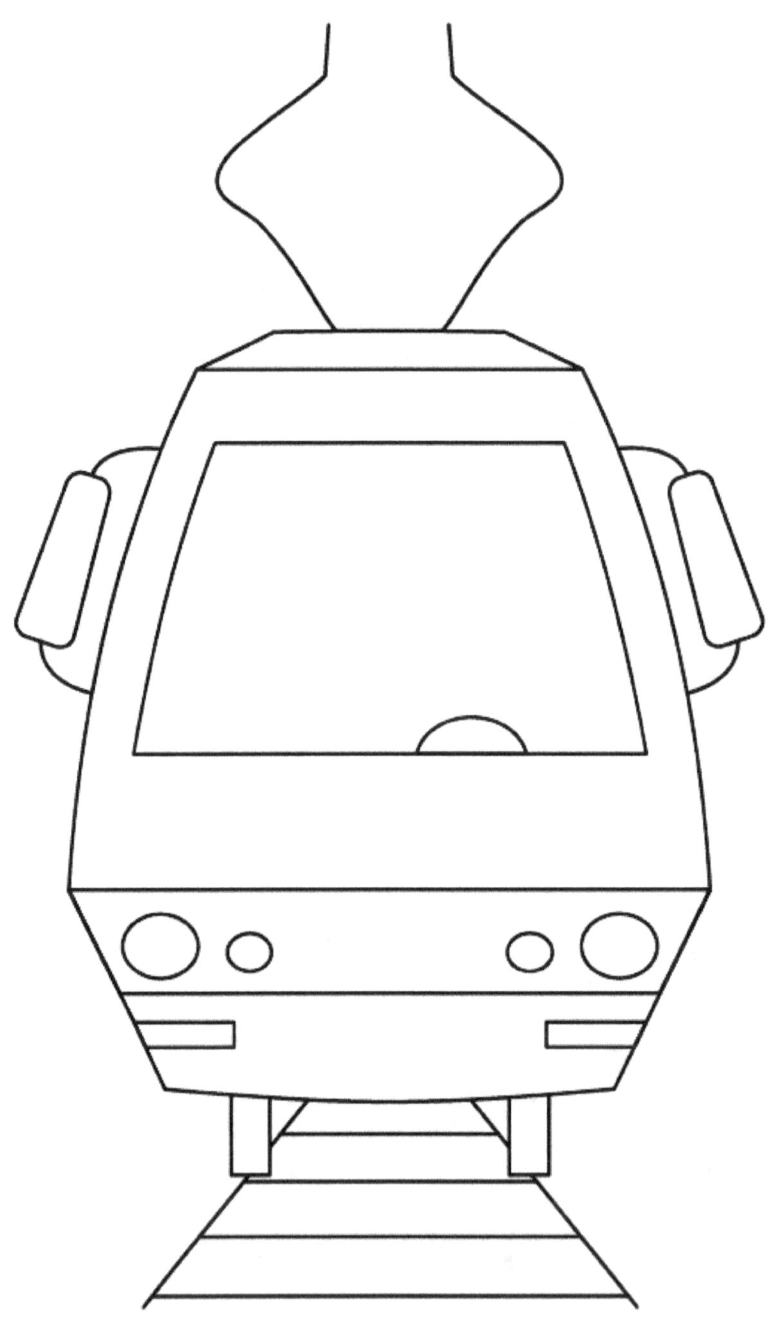

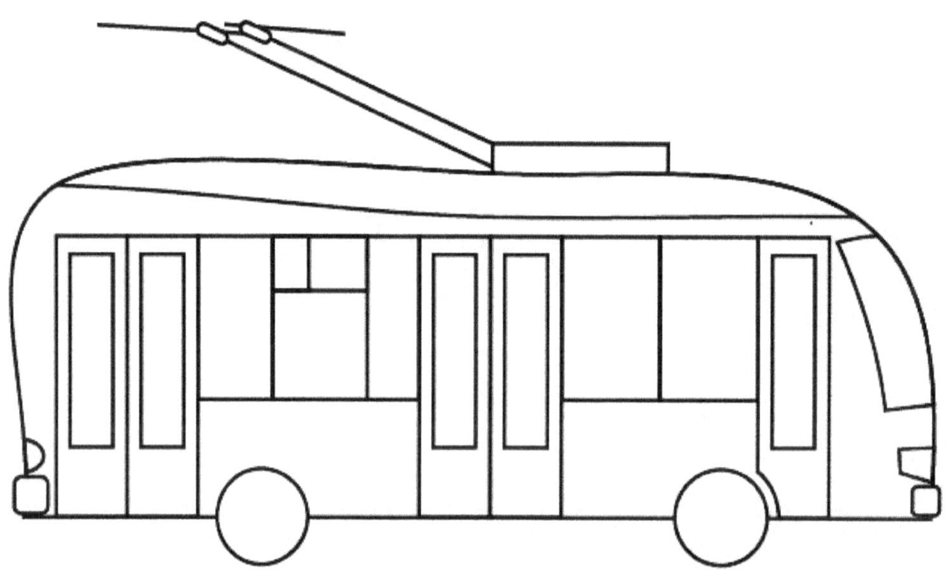

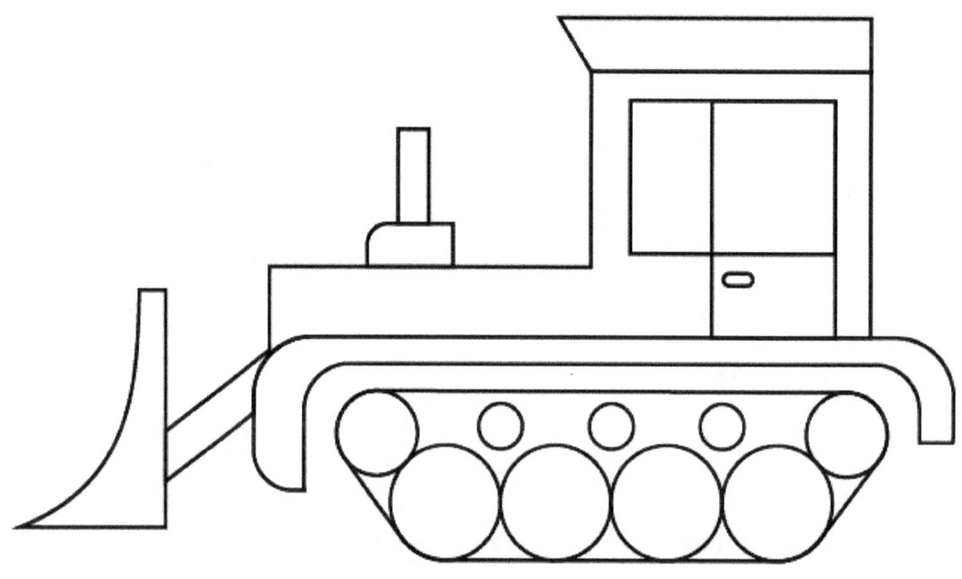

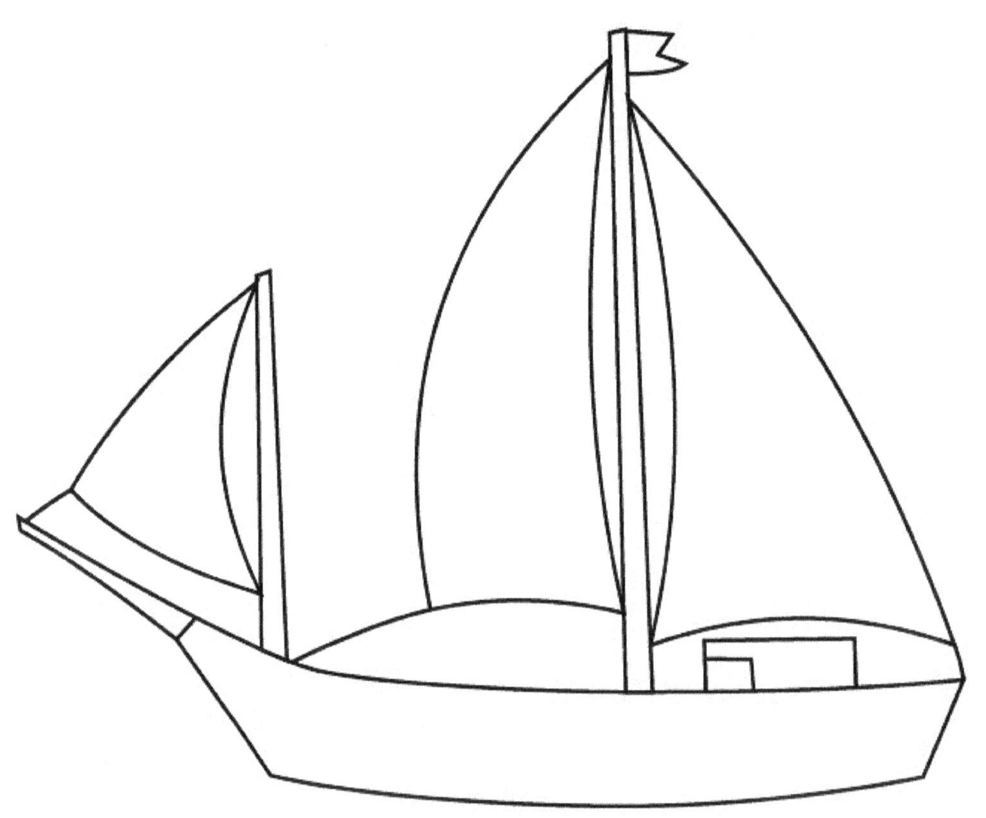

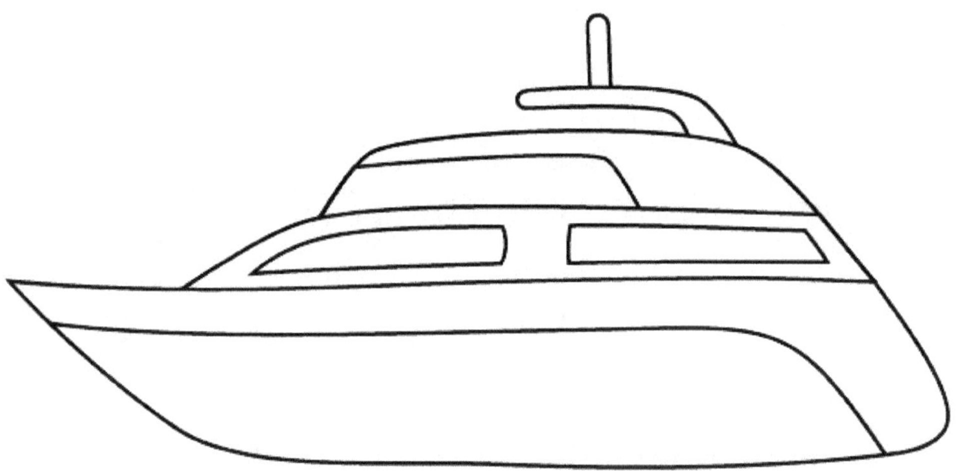

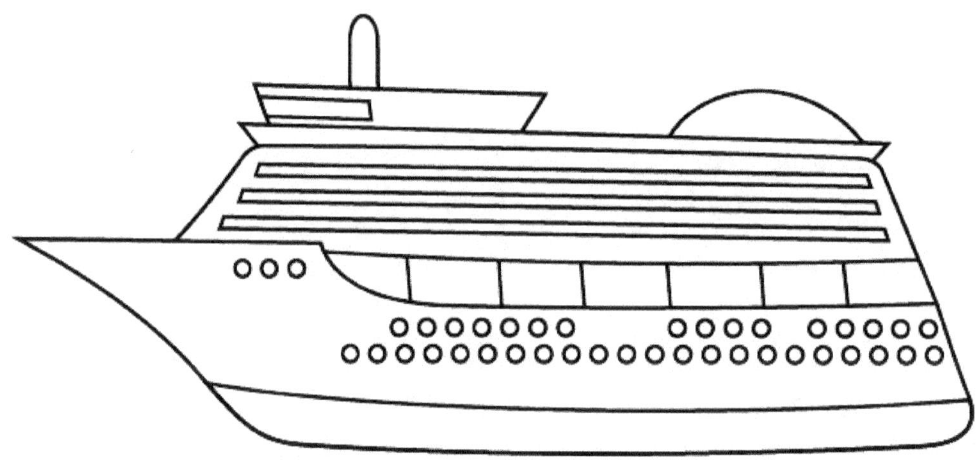

STOP